THEOTOKOS:

A *Via Media* for Anglicans

on the Subject of Mary

by

Dea. Lisa DellaVecchia

Theotokos: A Via Media for Anglicans on the Subject of Mary

A Theological Guidebook of the Praxeologion of Traditional Anglican Church of America

Written by Dea. Lisa DellaVecchia. Introduction by Rev. Canon Michael DellaVecchia.

The Jeremiad Christian Homesteaders Gazette, Publisher
Lisa DellaVecchia, Editor in Chief
Michael DellaVecchia, Publishing Director and Managing Editor

www.jeremiadchristianhomesteadersgazette.com

Authored and published by permission and under the guidance of Archbishop Rick Aaron Reid of Traditional Anglican Church of America

Winter Lenten Edition of *The Jeremiad Christian Homesteaders Gazette,*

Printed in the United States of America.

ISBN: 979-8-9889300-6-8

Introduction

By Rev. Canon Michael DellaVecchia

Why is Theotokos, the "God-bearer," important? No one is saved by praying to Mary through the Rosary (or by praying to any of the saints, for that matter). We pray to Christ alone. Truly, Mary is not the "co-redeemer." Her Son, Jesus, alone saves us; we truly need no one else but the Son of God. So how do we relate to His mother?

This Guidebook, devoted singularly to the subject of the Mother of God, is our special winter Lenten edition of the quarterly journal, *The Jeremiad Christian Homesteaders Gazette.* It serves as our Anglican testament to the profound theological significance of the Virgin Mother.

The very emotion that moves Christians to want to know the Virgin can be shared by anyone who has heartfelt adoration for their beloved—for their family, for their brethren. Pondering Mary's timeless and pure heart, along with its suffering, allows one to prayerfully reflect on the difficulties of the Christian life, especially considering the particular challenges of the modern world, with a quiet hope. Along with Mary, we can ponder these things in our hearts in a spirit of patience and faith.

Now, because certain questionable dogma concerning Mary (i.e., the "Immaculate Conception") became imposed upon Christendom in the late 1800s, the freedom that theologians had across the preceding centuries to contemplate her calling, her spirit, and her conception was replaced by an obligation to conform to a specific belief about Mary in order to remain a Roman Catholic. This was accomplished through the linguistic craft of the papal bull *Ineffabilis Deus*, written by Pius IX. By distorting and exaggerating the relevance of Mary for the Christian Faith, Pius IX caused faith in Christ to become shunted toward *worshipfulness*, if not actual worship, of Mary as the Immaculate Conception, one who had been "conceived without sin."

The permanent uplifting of womanhood, through Mary, that had been originally wrought by Jesus as the Savior and Son of God now became overtaken by a mindset that invoked harsh ecclesiastical rejection upon anyone who did not adopt the new institutionalized version of Mary. This counterfeit mockup of the Virgin was now a necessary lever believed by the indoctrinated to be necessary for Salvation. In the private lives of many, Mary became the central focus of devotion and prayer life. How did things get so far off track?

Deaconess Lisa DellaVecchia, the author of this Reformist book, has written theologically about Theotokos, placing her devotional relevance in its proper place— back in the heart of the believer, rather than in the psyche, where fear annihilates meditation and Hope. Thus, if you are a mother and you have felt the ecstasy of both sorrow and joy that Jesus's mother felt, then you will relate to this writing. The author herself has mothered six children, and being no stranger to the daily sorrows and joys felt by all parents (such as Mary), is moved to adore her own children, despite the significant challenges some of them face.

Whether you are a mother or a father, a parent or child, Traditional Anglicanism is able to give us the words by which the Mother of God should be heartfully contemplated: just as deeply as we think of and adore our own mothers, daughters, wives, sisters, and all of our children—and yet in a supernatural context as well.

Mary should have a proper, unmovable place—not ontologically (wherein one would be forced to see a her as made in a way that was different from that of all human mothers)—but in our hearts and souls as the Mother of God and *our* mother as well, throughout all of our days.

A *Via Media* for Anglicans on the Subject of Mary

In the lives of Christian people who "hunger and thirst after righteousness" (Matthew 5:6), there is quite often movement from one branch of Christianity to another, and even back again, in that lifelong quest to find the truest, most authentic, most Christ-pleasing expression of Christianity that human beings are capable of producing. Speaking from my own experience—one that is rather unique, and certainly involving more shifts along what I will call the "Christian continuum" than most people have ever done, or have ever wanted to do—that "hunger" of which Christ spoke in the beatitudes started when I was a very small child.

It started one day when I was sitting alone in my room, flipping through the illustrated pages of a children's Bible that my mother brought back from a trip to Israel. This was well before I knew anything of Christianity. Although this Bible did not include the New Testament, it opened up my young mind to God and His creation. I never tired of the stories and images presented in those pages; I still have the book, whose pages are yellow with age.

I was "raised Jewish"; I am half Jewish genetically but ethnically and culturally quite Jewish, since I never knew my birth father. The Jewish side of my family consisted of either atheistic-socialist, anti-Christian Jews on the one hand, or spiritually deprived non-religious (but *not* anti-Christian) Jews on the other. Not a single family member was religious in any way, but we liked to have family gatherings and eat on the Jewish holidays. It is against this backdrop that I can explain my movement toward Truth as I kept seeking, and finding, and knocking, and seeking again...and finding yet again.

When I was 10 years old, I almost went to a Yeshiva. My mother didn't want to send me to the local public school in Bayside, Queens, so she thought perhaps I should go to a Yeshiva, since Jewishness was really all she knew anything about at the time, even though said "Jewishness" was really only cultural, as it is for so many Jews. I was there when I heard the voice on the other end of the phone declining my mother's inquiry, on the grounds that I did not already speak Hebrew fluently. Heck, I didn't even know anything much about the Bible either, or the Torah, or anything about the rules and regulations of rabbinical Judaism, let alone speak Hebrew! That door closed, but my mother still wanted me out of the public school system.

Somehow I ended up at Redeemer Lutheran School on Bell Boulevard, the parochial school on the same campus as Redeemer Lutheran Church. Soon thereafter, at age 10, I was baptized, and this happy occasion was followed by my confirmation at age 12. It was at this school that I became an avid scholar of the Bible, attending Bible studies and holding my own with the grownups. The family joined that church right around this time, and my mother is still a Lutheran to this day.

I took a much different route from my mother, however. First I fell away from the church and Christ for a time, fancying myself an "atheist" from about the age of 16 until right around the time I was about to graduate from college. As for most kids, though the situation is so much bleaker today, these are the educational years during which all of the curriculum seems to make a concerted point to mock or discredit Christianity, the Bible, and the God of both.

But shortly after I graduated college and started working, I met a coworker who was openly Christian. She invited me to some Bible studies, and even though I was still very much steeped in the world, something started to change. I had the typical existential crisis that so many young people have experienced, and I came back to God literally on my hands and knees, weeping, at the age of about 22. In fact, my mother was the first person I called when it happened. The prayers of a mother—and I *know* she had been praying for me even though we never discussed it—are extremely powerful.

Very soon after attending these Bible studies, I started going to the same church that this office friend of mine went to, First Presbyterian Church in Philadelphia. And then even after I moved out of Philadelphia, I continued to attend some Presbyterian churches for a time. But there was something lacking for me in these churches—some things that weren't adding up. There are many issues with Calvinism that I will not get into here because that topic would be outside the scope of this discussion. Suffice it to say that a feeling like something was "off" theologically, combined with the ill treatment my autistic son and I received in the last Presbyterian church I went to before I left that denomination for good, catapulted me into the "catacombs" for a time.

I found myself in isolation with two young children, one of whom not only had a diagnosis of autism but also increasingly significant behavioral issues, plus an absentee-atheist husband who, it turned out later, was unfaithful to me, which was the biggest reason why the marriage ultimately ended. There I was, a young mother, originally a city girl, stuck in the suburbs with no church to go to, and no ability to receive any support for my faith from my then-husband, who was completely antagonistic to going to church at all, let alone believing in God.

In reaction, having no other options, I started an online group for parents with autism called Autistic Bible Church back in the late 1990s. As ridiculous as this may sound, I didn't know what else to do. It was through this online activity that I discovered Messianic Judaism. It made a lot of sense to me at the time, and it resonated with me for obvious reasons, but that, too, was a blind alley. I could go into the pitfalls of Messianic Judaism in another article.

After four years in the world of Messianic Judaism, I left it for good. I will say that I learned a lot from it though, just as I have learned a great deal from the other Christian paths I have taken. Every one of them had something of value to offer, as though each was looking at the same gemstone from different angles. Not all perspectives are equally worthy or palatable to everyone. But are we not all looking through a glass darkly?

> 12. For now we see through a glass, darkly; but then face to face to face: **now I know in part**; but then shall I know even as also I am known.
>
> *1 Corinthians 13:12*

Christians are human. We try. We don't always get everything right. But we are blessed to have a merciful God who knows our frailties and the motivations that drive our beliefs. That being said, there are some beliefs that *do not* pass muster and must be discarded. Certainly, beliefs with a Christian gloss that are patently heretical are automatically *anathema* and should never be adopted knowingly or willingly in the first place. However, there are grayer areas of belief that are not always easy to define as to what may be wrong with them. It may be that we can only evaluate their error by their fruits, and their fruits may not be known to a person until he or she is fully entrenched in them—rotten fruit that leads to less obvious ills, such as Phariseeism, spiritual gluttony, spiritual complacency, scrupulosity, attention diverted away from Christ, and the like.

More than my experience in the other mainline denominational churches, the experience I had in Messianic Judaism taught me that one can really start going way off course and yet still gain something of value. I learned that God sometimes, in His inscrutable wisdom, gives us a long leash and allows us to sniff around and collect "pollen" (i.e., various bits of truth) on our hides for a time, but when the time comes for those whom He loves, He gives us a tug and we come back to Him again. Or, to use the sheep metaphor of the Bible instead, He allows us to roam, but the time comes when

He calls and we hear His voice, and if we are His we come back to Him. "My sheep hear my voice, and I know them, and they follow me" (John 10:27).

As I mentioned earlier, my first marriage ended up in a divorce. But before that, in one last failed effort to save the marriage, I wanted us to have another child, and we did. That third child, a son, was born in 2001. By early 2004, it became evident not only that he had autism too, but that the impairments were much more profound than they were in his older brother. The marriage fell apart 3 years later on the grounds of infidelity.

I was blessed to have found someone new soon thereafter (you know him now as Rev. Canon Michael DellaVecchia) and remarried in 2008. Michael and I had the misfortune of ending up getting married in an awful Reconciling in Christ (RIC) Lutheran church with a female pastor and a liberal, worldly agenda. (As an aside, that church no longer exists; God will not be mocked.) I'm not proud to admit that I was already pregnant in my second trimester at the time, and we needed to get married *somewhere*. We thought that we could find a place that was entirely open to autistic children—by now we had *two* children with autism who could not sit through a church service—and this seemed like a place that was open minded enough that it could accommodate an unusual family like ours. Needless to say that that experience, too, went up in flames, and not just "because autism." I will not get into the reasons why I got up one day and walked out of that church, never to return. Anyone familiar with the agendas that have infested the churches today need not have the reasons explained.

Not long after we as a family withdrew from that church, I ended up converting to Roman Catholicism. My new husband was a cradle Catholic, so the thought was that this would put us both on the same religious ground, and Catholicism seemed to have what I had been seeking all along: authenticity, historical legitimacy, clear rules, sacraments, tales of saints and heroes, and the like. Becoming Catholic felt like being in another spiritual plane for a time, like being absorbed into a vast ocean of rightness that made everything make sense. Since I thought that I had finally found what I had been seeking, I became an über-Catholic, learning everything I possibly could learn about it, becoming extremely devout, saying my Rosary daily, and even refusing to wear pants, but only wearing long skirts, because it wasn't "Mary-like" to wear pants. We didn't eat meat on Fridays; we observed Holy Days of Obligation. We wore brown scapulars. We kneeled during the Eucharist while everyone else in the Novus Ordo churches we attended gave us the side eye and snickered. Then, when we couldn't stand it any longer to participate in the Novus Ordo farce, we started looking for Traditional Catholic churches, only to find that there was no home for us there either.

In 2015, two years into Pope Francis's pontificate, we became Sedevacantists, doubling down on our Traditional Catholicism by becoming Ultramontanists and insisting that Pope Francis was no pope at all, but was in fact a heretic, thus making his seat "vacant." There was nowhere to go; we had painted ourselves into a corner. Even the "Trad" church we finally found within 2 hours of our house was a disaster: one Sunday we got ourselves dressed to the nines and dragged all our kids to a Mass there, whereupon the priest literally used his bully pulpit to yell at the congregation to listen to Francis and stop being so "unloving" by taking issue with his radical agenda. We scooped up all the kids and walked out in the middle of the Mass.

We were thrust back into our home again, with nowhere to go and nobody who could possibly understand the spiritual and practical (e.g., due to autism) turmoil we were experiencing. I had the old familiar sensation of being back in the catacombs, running that Autistic Bible Church on the Internet in a desperate attempt to find other Christians who were in my same position.

We were in an absolutely ridiculous predicament. Roman Catholicism had run its course and could not be cured. There was no turning back the clocks, and the more I read about and dissected Catholicism, the more I realized that the clocks had to keep being turned back more and more. Would it be okay to turn the clocks back to before Vatican II? Nope. How about before Vatican I? Nope. What about before Trent? Not really. How far back did the clock have to be turned until the teachings and practices of the Catholic Church began to legitimately look and feel more like the Church that Christ actually built? I studied Church history and the patristic writings extensively at around this time, and all of those studies pulled me in the direction of the Orthodox Church.

So we turned as a family to Orthodoxy. I didn't, and I still don't, have any problem with the Orthodox Church, but there was no place for us there. We tried. The extreme autism on the part of one of our children, whose symptoms intensified the older he got and the larger he grew, ended up precluding us from going anywhere—I mean *anywhere*—as a family to worship publicly.

And it's as though God designed it that way, because soon after entering the Orthodox Church (but with only *some* of us being able to go at any given time, putting a strain on our family), my husband's lifelong calling to the priesthood began to tug at his heart. He entered into priestly studies under a senior Orthodox Bishop, but a grievous falling out eventually occurred. The church to which we had belonged, as it turned out, was in fact a most tragically unorthodox place. Moreover, the rector of the church died not long after we left, which we only on discovered after we had moved out of Montgomery County.

We moved to Bucks County in 2020 and tried to settle into a different Orthodox church in the area, much closer to our new home, but we were met with a whole new crop of challenges and signals that we were not wanted there.

We were in the wilderness again, but conversely the calling to the priesthood became stronger and stronger. As our readership knows, my husband ended up in the Traditional Anglican Church of America and *did* after all become ordained as a priest, fulfilling the irresistible calling of the Holy Spirit. He is now Reverend Canon, Rector of St. Patricks' Anglican Church, and head of the TACA Diocese of the Northeast under Archbishop Rick Aaron Reid.

This is where our family is comfortably and blessedly today, and this story shows the parallel development of a family's spiritual journey on the one hand and its journey with autism on the other. In fact, it was autism that provided the humble catalyst at every juncture as to whether we should turn to the right or turn to the left. One shouldn't discount life's various challenges; maybe yours isn't autism but something else that makes the world reject you. God knows what He's doing.

Because of this decades-long movement along the Christian continuum, we have collected a lot of "pollen" on our backs. By the grace of God we have kept the good and discarded whatever is evil, false, or merely unfruitful.

What, you might ask, was the point of taking up all of these pages to describe such a winding spiritual path? I was asked by my husband to write an article on Mary. This is a heady and difficult topic. How can a Christian write intelligently about Mary unless he or she first of all has done a lot of studying and thinking about her, and unless he or she has experienced Mary in a variety of different contexts? I believe that my circuitous path, as described earlier in this article, puts me in a position of being able to look at Mary thoughtfully and objectively.

I will not regurgitate thoughts about Mary—from one extreme to the opposite—as given to me by various sources over the years, taking one side or the other by way of coming down in favor of one view or the other. Instead, my goal in embarking on this study journey is to engage in a discovery along with you and seeing where we end up on the other side.

Throughout my life I have run the gamut when it comes to Mary: I have ignored Mary as utterly irrelevant to me, and I have prayed to Mary in decades upon decades of the Rosary daily. As a member of the Orthodox Church, my devotion to Mary somewhat waned, since there is not *as* great of an emphasis on Mary as there is in Roman Catholicism. Though my attention to Mary has certainly mellowed in recent years, icons of Mary remain on our walls, never to be taken down. Her image, together with images of Christ, the angels, and the saints, are placed in positions of honor in our home and in our church.

But what to *do* with Mary is the question. Who is she? Is she just another saint and disciple among all the others? Was she just a flawed human vessel whose "use" was fulfilled at Christ's birth? We shouldn't be surprised that an understanding of Mary is such a mystery to so many. It's why the song *Mary, Did You Know?* is so popular around Christmastime, even though some people hate it, scoffing at the ridiculous question. "Of course she knew!" they retort. Clearly Christians are divided on the question of Mary. For this reason, a study of Mary and guidelines for approaching her are sorely needed in our Anglican churches. My goal is to develop in these pages a sound approach to Marian teaching for the Traditional Anglican Church of America.

If you are still reading, then it's probably safe to say that you have been curious as to how we as Christians should see her. Maybe you adore the *Ave Maria* sung at Christmastime, but as an Anglican, you don't know if you *should*. Have you ever wondered if we should refer to Mary as the Blessed Mother, or does that sound too Roman Catholic? Is she really the Immaculate Conception, as the Catholics claim? What does the "Immaculate Conception" mean, and should this term really refer to Mary at all? Is Mary really *our* mother? Is it appropriate to pray *to* Mary, which is what Catholics are actually doing when they recite the Rosary? Is Mary just another saint or is she more than a saint? Should we look only to the Bible to figure out how to see Mary, or should we also look at Sacred Tradition, including apocryphal texts, the writings of the Church Fathers, early Christian art, and so forth, to come to a right understanding?

As you can see, the question of "who is Mary?" is a very difficult one. It is difficult to peel away one's particular Faith Tradition for the purpose of investigating her. Depending on who and what she is, it may be entirely irrelevant and inconsequential to have a right understanding of her, or it may actually be vital to know her and be a part of her. Or it could be that the reality is somewhere in between, but that will be for you to decide when you get to the end of this article.

Probably the most frustrating part in trying to understand Mary lies in the fact that she says so little in the Bible, where she speaks only four times: (1) in conversing with the Angel Gabriel (Luke 1:34, 38); (2) in speaking with her cousin Elisabeth and praying what we refer to as the Magnificat (Luke 1:46-55); (3) in admonishing Jesus when she and Joseph could not find Him for three days (Luke 2:48); and (4) in the wedding feast at Cana, when in anticipation of His first miracle, she instructs the servants, "Whatsoever He saith unto you, do it" (John 3:5).

Mary is mentioned, however, in many other places in the New Testament outside of those passages where she speaks. She is there for the presentation of Christ in the

Temple. She is there at the foot of the cross. She is there in the upper room at Pentecost. Clearly her presence is a constant throughout the Gospels and into the book of Acts, but then her presence drops off—or does it? Some have argued that since Mary is not mentioned in any of the Epistles, Mary must not be a significant part of Christianity at all, since she is not foundational to the right understanding of Christian doctrine. This makes for an interesting case, but then we have the Book of Revelation, where "the woman" is described. Who is she?

1. And there appeared a great wonder in heaven; a woman clothed with the sun, and the moon under her feet, and upon her head a crown of twelve stars:
2. And she being with child cried, travailing in birth, and pained to be delivered.
3. And there appeared another wonder in heaven; and behold a great red dragon, having seven heads and ten horns, and seven crowns upon his heads.
4. And his tail drew the third part of the stars of heaven, and did cast them to the earth; and the dragon stood before the woman which was ready to be delivered,

for to devour her child as soon as it was born.

5. And she brough forth a man child, **who was to rule all nations with a rod of iron**: and her child was caught up to God, and to his throne.

6. And the woman fled into the wilderness, where she hath a place prepared of God, that they should feed her there a thousand two hundred and threescore days...

13. And when the dragon saw that **he was cast unto the earth**, he persecutest the woman which brought forth the man child.

14. And to the woman were given two wings of a great eagle, that she might fly into the wilderness, into her place, where she is nourished for a time, and times, and half a time, from the face of the serpent.

15. And the serpent cast out of his mouth water as a flood after the woman, that he might cause her to be carried away of the flood.

16. And the earth helped the woman, and the earth opened up her mouth, and swallowed up the flood which the dragon cast out of his mouth.

17. And the dragon was wroth with the woman, **and went to make war with the remnant of her seed**, which keep the commandments of God, and have the testimony of Jesus Christ.

Revelation 12:1-6, 13-17

Now, the Roman Catholic Church interprets the "woman clothed with the sun" to be Mary herself—not merely an allegorical symbol of Israel or the Church, as is often taught in Protestant circles. Let's take a look at the clues within this passage to see if the Roman Catholic view holds up under scrutiny:

Clue #1: The man child "was to rule all nations with a rod of iron" (verse 5). Has either Israel or the Church ever ruled "all nations with a rod of iron"? Absolutely not. This test fails. Who is the only figure ever promised to "rule all nations with a rod of iron"? That person is Christ Jesus Himself and no other.

Jesus declares earlier in Revelation that He will share the power He *already has* to rule the nations with a "rod of iron" with those who keep His works:

26. And he that overcometh, and keepeth my works unto the end, to him will I give power over the nations: 27. And he shall rule them **with a rod of iron**; as the vessels of a potter shall they be broken to shivers: **even as I received of my Father**.

Revelation 2:26-27

And how do we know that Christ is the One who is being referred to in Revelation 12, in that the power to rule the nations is His and one that He will share with those who remain faithful to Him until the end? We know by this:

12. His eyes were as a flame of fire, and on his head were many crowns; and he had a name written, that no man knew but he himself. 13. And he was clothed with a vesture dipped in blood: and his name is called The Word of God. 14. And the armies which were in heaven followed him upon white horses, clothed in fine linen, white and clean. 15. And out of his mouth goeth a sharp sword, that with it he should

smite the nations: and **he shall rule them with a rod of iron**: and he treadeth the winepress of the fierceness and wrath of Almighty God.

Revelation 19:12-15

Throughout the Psalms and Isaiah especially, with examples too great to enumerate here, we have further evidence that Christ Himself will rule and reign as King of Kings over the nations, judging rightly, bringing a period of peace in what is known as the Millennial Kingdom, and ruling "all nations" with a rod of iron. In fact "They that dwell in the wilderness shall bow before him; and his enemies shall lick the dust ... Yea, **all kings shall fall down before him: all nations shall serve him**" (Psalm 72:9, 11). This is what is actually meant by the words of the Lord's Prayer: "Thy kingdom come, Thy will be done." Right now, kings rule this world under the power of the prince of this world (John 16:11), but it will not always be so.

Clues #2 and #3: There is a connection between the "woman clothed with the sun" (Revelation 12) and Eve (Genesis 3). The same dragon that persecuted the "woman clothed with the sun" and her "man child" is the one who was "cast unto the earth" (Revelation 12) and seduced Eve to sin against God. The same serpent-dragon "went to make war with" the physical children of Eve (mankind in general) and with the spiritual children of Mary (Christians). Christians are the "remnant of **her** [*who is she?*] seed, which keep the commandments of God, and have the testimony of Jesus Christ" (Revelation 12).

Now then, the "woman clothed with the sun" can be none other than Mary for this reason: the "man child" in Revelation 12 can be none other than Jesus Christ. There, too, is a connection clearly drawn between the seed of Eve and the seed of Mary, and for this reason there is a connection between Eve and Mary *spiritually*, which the Roman Catholics as well as the Orthodox have discerned long ago.

Even the term "the woman" is interesting: in Revelation 12 "the woman" is used mysteriously, but I believe it is for a purpose: that term is supposed to capture both Eve and Mary at the same time, but in two different senses. Are Mary and Eve to be considered one and the same by way of the term "the woman"? No, but the "seed" concept is quite interesting, and I'll explain why I believe that the two women seem to blend into one by verse 17 of Revelation 12.

Taking a detour for a moment, let's look at how God Himself describes fruits and seeds in the Creation narrative:

> 11. And God said, Let the earth bring forth grass, the herb yielding seed, and the fruit tree yielding fruit after his kind, **whose seed is in itself**, upon the earth: and it was so.

> *Genesis 1:11*

Every fruit carries the seed of the next generation of fruit inside of itself. Likewise, Eve carried within herself the seed of all future generations, including Mary. And so, in a sense, Mary was *already present* in Eve, before Mary existed physically.

And so the term "the woman," which by the end of Revelation 12 seems to blend Eve and Mary together, as two sides of the same coin, being united by the fact that the serpent wants to see both of them and their "seed" destroyed, begins to make sense, and a theological concept begins to emerge. The enigmatic "Woman," which is how Jesus addresses His mother at the foot of the cross, begins to make even more sense in this light.

> When Jesus therefore saw his mother, and the disciple standing by, whom he loved, he saith unto his mother, Woman, behold thy son!

> *John 19:26*

A statement is being made by Jesus's use of "Woman." But what?

In Genesis 3, after Eve fell and caused Adam to fall as well, God declares a curse upon the serpent, Satan:

> 15. And I will put enmity between thee and the woman, and **between thy seed and her seed**; it shall bruise thy head, and thou shalt bruise his heel.

> *Genesis 3:15*

Now let's look again at Revelation 12:17 and put it all together:

17. And the dragon was wroth with the woman, and went to make war **with the remnant of her seed, which keep the commandments of God**, and have the testimony of Jesus Christ.

We can safely say that Christ is Mary's physical "seed," since Christ is in truth the "man child" whom she bore, but we also learn that Christians are her "seed" as well, because Christians are the ones who are the "remnant," the ones who "keep the commandments of God, and have the testimony of Jesus Christ" and are being persecuted by Satan until the end. So if Christ is Mary's seed, and Mary is His mother, and if we are Mary's seed too, then Mary is our mother too, but in a spiritual sense. We are children of Eve in a *physical* sense, but we are children of Mary in a *spiritual* sense.

Does this analysis, if true, square with other parts of Sacred Scripture? Let's take a look. Does it make sense to believe that Christians—those who "keep the commandments of God, and have the testimony of Jesus Christ" are the "seed" of Mary, which would make her our mother in a spiritual sense? There is a passage in all three synoptic Gospels that can be taken in two different ways, depending on one's bias: one in which Jesus seems to be disavowing and rebuking the significance of His mother, and another in which Jesus is using a situation to teach a spiritual truth, and to elevate the physical realm to the spiritual realm (i.e., to draw a spiritual or abstract principle from something that is concrete and finite). Take a look at this passage:

> 46. While he yet talked to the people, behold, his mother and his brethren stood without, desiring to speak with him.
> 47. Then one said unto him, Behold, thy mother and thy brethren stand without, desiring to speak with thee.
> 47. But he answered and said unto him that told him, Who is my mother? and who are my brethren?
> 49. And he stretched forth his hand toward his disciples, and said, Behold my mother and my brethren!
> 50. For whosoever shall do the will of my Father which is in heaven, the same is my brother, and sister, and mother.

> *Matthew 12:46-50*

If your bias is that Mary was not very important to Jesus or to the Faith, that Jesus had other physical brothers born of Mary, and they were all standing outside, perhaps trying to prevent Him from teaching, then you will likely interpret this passage on one end of the extreme: that Jesus was arguing that it was not worth His time to leave the house where He was teaching simply to talk to His mother and brethren (in other words, that the disciples seated around him were more important and more worthy than His mother and His brethren because *they* were listening to Him whereas his mother and brethren were *not*). The problem is that we have no evidence to support that conclusion:

1. There is no support for the notion that His mother and His brethren were not disciples (in fact, we know for certain that they *were* disciples).
2. The fact that they were "standing without" does not prove that they were against Jesus's teaching or were removing themselves from His instruction. They could have simply just gotten there and wanted to tell Him something urgently.

3. There is no evidence that Jesus was exposing His mother and brethren as not doing "the will of the Father."

4. The Bible is completely silent on whether, moments after Jesus made this statement, He actually *did* leave the house to find out what they wanted to tell him. Do we not know that Jesus obeyed His mother? When He was found to be in Jerusalem after having gone missing for three days, He "went down with them, and came to Nazareth, **and was subject unto them**" (Luke 2:51a).

So you can see how one's bias can cause one to draw a particular conclusion about a Mary passage simply according to what one may have been taught. Let's take another very similar example. Again in Luke, there is a passage that reads thusly:

27. And it came to pass, as he spake these things, a certain woman of the company lifted up her voice, and said unto him, Blessed is the womb that bare thee, and the paps which thou has sucked.

33

28. But he said, **Yea rather**, blessed are they that hear the word of God, and keep it.

Luke 11:27-28

Now again, as with the previous passage, this certainly seems like Jesus is contradicting the woman who poured out this praise upon Mary. It certainly seems like Jesus is saying, "Do not call Mary blessed" and/or "only those who hear the word of God and keep it are blessed" or even—shockingly—"Mary does not hear or keep the word of God and for that reason cannot be called blessed."

Obviously, these interpretations are ludicrous, and so taking this passage combined with the previous passage in which Jesus refers to all who listen to Him as His "mother and brothers," we must ask ourselves: what is He doing? What does He mean? Could He really be slamming His mother? Does this even make any sense?

No, it does not make sense. Mary prophesied in the Magnificat, saying, "for, behold, from henceforth all generations shall call me blessed" (Luke 1:48). So what is happening, and why have generations of Christians been taught the anti-Mary position that Jesus was rebuking anyone who gave Mary any relevance or honor or special position of blessedness? But wait, one may object: aren't we *all* blessed, as Christians? Yes, we are, but does that make us *equal* in blessedness to Mary? Decide for yourself by examining the words of Saint Elisabeth:

> 41. And it came to pass, that, when Elisabeth heard the salutation of Mary, the babe leaped in her womb; and Elisabeth was **filled with the Holy Ghost**:
> 42. **And she spake** out with a loud voice, and said, "Blessed art **thou among women**, and blessed is the **fruit** of thy womb.
> 43. And whence is this to me, that **the mother of my Lord** should come to me?
> 44. For, lo, as soon as the voice of thy salutation sounded in mine ears, the babe leaped in my womb for joy.
> 45. And **blessed is she that believed**: for there shall be a performance of those things **which were told her from the Lord**.

> *Luke 1:41-45*

Mary's faith, her special honor, her special blessedness, as proclaimed in a loud voice by Saint Elisabeth through the inspiration of the Holy Ghost, never changed or dissipated. She was one of the few disciples who stood at the foot of the cross and endured the torture of watching her dear Son be put to death in the cruelest possible way, not fleeing like a coward—not concerned that she, too, might also be put to death for following Jesus. And so we *cannot* assume that Jesus is taking a position of rebuke in the above two passages (Matthew 12 and Luke 11). What is happening then?

What is happening is that Jesus is using both examples as a teaching moment. He wishes to shift the focus away from the physical world to the more perfect invisible and spiritual world. After all, do we not declare in the Apostle's Creed that we believe in the "visible **and** invisible"?

In the first instance, Jesus is not demoting His mother and brethren as being non-disciples. In fact, He is turning the whole situation on its head: He is elevating the disciples with whom He is speaking to the spiritual position of His "mother and brethren," who have *never lost* their position to begin with, by virtue of their faith. He is bringing the disciples gathered around him deeper into His own fold, as opposed to turning away His mother and brethren. Likewise in the second instance, Jesus is not implying that Mary should be discounted and ignored because of unbelief. Quite the contrary: Jesus is saying that we should not focus on the physical aspects of the human womb that bore Him and the human paps that gave Him suck, but should instead focus on the *fiat* of Mary: "And Mary said, Behold the handmaid of the Lord; be it done unto me according to thy word" (Luke 1:38). Jesus is saying here that what is worthy of praise and adulation is the *faith* of Mary, which cannot be disputed, and not on the physical mechanics of her having given birth to the Savior.

After all, it is not by the *birth* of Christ that we are saved, but it is by faith *in* Christ that we are saved. "For by grace are ye saved through faith; and that not of yourselves: it is the gift of God" (Ephesians 2:8). Christ, in issuing the seeming "rebuke" in the second passage, draws this important distinction— one that should help prevent the rather indulgent practice of focusing on various body parts of Christ and Mary and turning them into devotionals, sacramentals, and objects of near-worship (e.g., the "Sacred Heart" and the "Immaculate Heart of Mary") so common in Roman Catholic circles. As Christians, we are to understand that faith and obedience are of primary importance, whereas the body—though certainly not nothing, as certain heretics would hold—is of *lesser* importance while still holding a place of high position.[1] Jesus said, "It is the spirit that quickeneth; **the flesh profiteth nothing**: the words that I speak unto you, *they* are spirit, and *they* are life" (John 6:63).

Let us conclude this first part by looking again at the same passage cited earlier, but turning our attention to the Apostle John: the one whom Jesus loved, the one who with Mary the mother of Our Lord stood at the foot of the cross, and the one whom Jesus commanded take Mary as His own mother.

―――――――――――――――

[1] However, our bodies are quite important too, and we as Christians must keep our bodies holy: "What? Know ye not that your body is the temple of the Holy Ghost which is in you, which ye have of God, and ye are not your own? For ye are bought with a price: therefore glorify God in your body, and in your spirit, which are God's" (1 Corinthians 6:19-20).

26. When Jesus therefore saw his mother, and the disciple standing by, whom he loved, he saith unto his mother, Woman, behold thy son!
27. Then saith he to the disciple, Behold thy mother! And from that hour that disciple took her unto his own.

John 19:26-27

It was this same apostle who wrote these words:

1. Behold, what manner of love the Father hath bestowed upon us, that we should be called the sons of God: therefore the world knoweth us not, because it knew him not.

1 John 3:1

What we have here is something happening in the visible, physical realm (like the womb and paps of Mary) being transported into the more perfect spiritual realm: Practically speaking, the Apostle John *has* become the literal, actual brother of Christ by physical adoption. Mary *is* now John's mother, and John is to take Mary into his home and care for her as his own mother. Since then John has at this very moment become Jesus's actual adoptive brother, does that make all of us Jesus's brothers and sisters as well, in that John is acting as a representative or model for the rest of us Christians, and if so, wouldn't that make Mary *our* mother too? John said that we are all the "sons of God" (John 1:12, 1 John 3:1) through faith, but is his teaching supported elsewhere in the Bible?

The concept of adoption is used throughout the Epistles, and it shows truly how our relationship to Jesus Christ evolved first from servants to friends in the Gospels, then to an emerging understanding toward the end of the Gospels of being brought into His own family, to the full-blown concept fleshed out in the Epistles of being "sons of God" through the Holy Spirit, as we read:

2. Grace be to you, and peace, from God our Father, and from the Lord Jesus Christ.
3. **Blessed be the God and Father of** our Lord Jesus Christ, who hath blessed us with all spiritual blessings in heavenly places in Christ:

4. According as **he hath chosen us** in him before the foundation of the world, that we should be holy and without blame before him in love:

5. **Having predestinated us unto the adoption of children by Jesus Christ to himself**, according to the good pleasure of his will,

6. To the praise of the glory of his grace, **wherein he hath made us accepted in the beloved**.

Ephesians 1:2-6

Both the Roman Catholic and Orthodox Churches share the appropriate understanding of who Mary is and who we are in relation to her: Mary is our mother by the spirit of adoption, we His disciples are one family with Mary the Mother of God (*Theotokos*) and with His brethren, that it is faith that binds us together as one, that Mary is blessed among women (i.e., that although we are all blessed, Mary is given the particular blessing and honor of being the Mother of God, an honor that no other woman has ever shared), that Mary is the "woman clothed with the sun," that Mary has a special relation to Eve, as we shall see, and that Mary is truly a very important figure whom we should contemplate with reverence and love.

It does no damage to the integrity of Traditional Anglicanism to share these same beliefs with our Roman Catholic and Orthodox brethren in Christ. In fact, these beliefs are as ancient as the Church herself. "The earliest recorded prayer to Mary is the *sub suum praesidium* (3rd or 4th century) and the earliest depictions of her are from the Pricilla catacombs in Rome. Clearly the impulse to give Mary high honor and praise is ancient and occurred much earlier than the religious abuses of Rome that gave rise to the Great Schism, followed five centuries later by the Protestant Reformation.

Ironically, the novelty here is actually the modern notion that Mary is of no consequence and should simply be ignored like any other woman, or maybe just brought out of the closet like a trinket and dusted off on Christmas, as an act of quaint sentimentality but certainly not reverence. However, even if it could be said that we as Traditional Anglicans share the same Marian position with our Apostolic Church brethren, where we must differ—especially with

Rome—is in terms of the *expression* of that belief and the lengths to which we are willing to take it in both mind and spiritual practice.

Speaking to the knee-jerk aversion to anything Marian at all among Protestant circles, how is it that we have no problem calling a mere priest "Reverend," but we have problems revering Mary? This is only one small example among many of the various hypocritical stances that people take (not unlike the stance against statues and the mass—unless it is Christmas[s]!). Such aversion to Mary on the part of so many Christians is a counterreaction that formed on the part of Protestants—and rightly so— against the overemphasis on Mary in the salvation story and the worshipful attention paid to her on the part of the Roman Catholic Church. In my walk back and forth along the Christian continuum, I have seen no regard whatsoever paid to Mary in modern-day Lutheranism or Presbyterianism, let alone Messianic Judaism. I do think it's interesting, though, to read what Luther thought of Mary. In fact, he held her in very high esteem, higher than all of the saints, considering her worthy of *hyperdulia,* as Catholics and Orthodox also contend.

Luther wrote: "[S]he became the Mother of God, in which work so many and such great good things are bestowed on her as pass man's understanding. For on this there follows all honor, all blessedness, and her unique place in the whole of mankind, among which she has no equal, namely that she had a child by the Father in heaven....It needs to be pondered in the heart what it means to be the Mother of God" (*Luther's Works*, 21:326).

Calvin was not as sanguine when it came to his opinion of the Blessed Mother, but he did refer to her quite liberally as "the Virgin" and did consider her the Mother of God, even though he wished to suppress common usage of the term, so as not to cause a stumbling-block to the "ignorant" and to confirm them in their "superstitions" (*Letters of John Calvin*, Volume 1, Dr. Jules Bonnet, Editor, 2007).

So what are we as Anglican Christians to believe about Mary based on the evidence that can be found in Sacred Scripture and Sacred Tradition? As with so many things, moderation is key. It is incumbent upon

Traditional Anglicans to extend the concept of the *via media*—a concept that literally means the "middle road" between two extremes, as, for instance, between Protestantism and Roman Catholicism—to Mary as well. Is there a middle road that can be followed when it comes to our relationship with Mary? I believe so.

Before we examine that question, we might want to look first at the concepts regarding Mary that have developed *beyond* the ones that can be derived from Sacred Scripture by simple inference, as I have done in the preceding pages. In other words, the concept that Mary is our mother by virtue of the fact that we are very brothers of Christ (i.e., that God the Father adopts us as His sons through Christ Jesus) is fairly easy to deduce.

There are deeper interpretations of Mary, however, that theologians have developed over the centuries that are to my mind even richer and more compelling than the obvious ones. After all, is it not a hard leap of faith to believe that we are one family with Christ and His human family by adoption, and that we are also one family with Christ as the Head of the Body, the spiritual Church—one body with Him, knitted together. The unity of all believers goes on continuously on earth and in heaven. We gather together for worship as one body on Sundays, and we are also united with the whole company of heaven together with God in the Communion of Saints, which we confess to believe in our Creed. It's not difficult to believe and understand that Mary is our mother and the mother of the Church. It stands to reason that she is.

There are even deeper depths to be plumbed about Mary, however, which are worthy of serious consideration. If you are not a Traditional Catholic, you probably are not aware that there is a longstanding tradition of considering Mary to be the "New Eve" and "New Ark [of the Covenant]". She is also considered to be the Queen Mother, whom the King "cannot refuse." All of these concepts come from—you guessed it—the Bible, but they are ones you have to really dig around for if you haven't already stumbled upon them in your readings of the Church Fathers. Let's look at all three.

Mary as the New Eve

Although the Bible does not explicitly refer to Mary as "the New Eve" the foundation for the idea that the fall of man was "flipped" in the salvation story was certainly lain by the very biblical concept of Christ as the "New Adam," as we read:

14. Nevertheless death reigned from Adam to Moses, even over them that had not sinned after the similitude of Adam's transgression, who is the figure of him that was to come...
17. For if by one man's offence death reigned by one; much more they which receive abundance of grace and of the gift of righteousness shall reign in life by one, Jesus Christ.)
18. Therefore as by the offence of one judgment came upon all men to condemnation; even so by the righteousness of one the free gift came upon all men unto justification of life.
19. For as by one man's disobedience many were made sinners, so by the obedience of one shall many be made righteous.

Romans 5:14, 17-19

21. For since by man came death, by man came also the resurrection of the dead. 22. For as in Adam all die, even so in Christ shall all be made alive.

1 Corinthians 15:21-21

The Church Fathers believed the same "flipping of the script" applied to Mary as well—and why wouldn't it? It stands to reason that it would. As Saint Jerome characteristically put it so succinctly, "Death came through Eve, but life has come through Mary" (St. Jerome, *Epistle 22*, 21).

Eve succumbed most woefully to the "lust of the eyes" and the "pride of life" against which we are to this day warned (1 John 2:16), disobediently eating that which was forbidden, showing through her pride and ingratitude a spirit of rebellion, obeying the foreign voice of one who played no part in her creation, and wanting to usurp the bounds placed between God and mankind—you can go here, but no further—bounds placed for our protection and not for our harm, like guardrails on a highway rimmed on both sides by cliffs. Eve's faithlessness and disobedience was mirrored inversely by Mary's faithfulness and obedience in her *fiat* in response to the Angel Gabriel: "be it unto me according to thy word"—Luke 1:38.

Three attributes can be gleaned from Mary's response to Gabriel (in contradistinction to Eve's response to that other angelic being, the fallen Lucifer): (1) she *believed* the words that Gabriel spoke, (2) she *obeyed* the will of God, and (3) she *lowered* herself, considering herself to be the humble handmaid of the Lord (i.e., she did not puff herself up; she did not fill herself up with pride at having been uniquely chosen to be the Mother of God).

Likewise, Justin Martyr wrote the following, in *Dialogue with Trypho*:

"[Jesus] became man by the Virgin, in order that the disobedience which proceeded from the serpent might receive its destruction in the same manner in which it derived its origin. For Eve, who was a virgin and undefiled, having conceived the word of the serpent, brought forth disobedience and death."

Centuries of contemplation by Christian theologians from the inception of the Church starting in the 100s A.D. to today have led to the conclusion that Mary is in fact a very integral part of the salvation story. As the saying goes, "No Mary, no Christ; know Mary, know Christ." While this saying may sound like a bit of a stretch, and "awfully *Catholic*," if you think about it, it's true! While the Son of God as the second person of the Holy Trinity is God Himself, the eternal Word—"and the Word was with God, and the Word was God" (John 1:1)—at the same time Jesus Christ, who is God Incarnate, became so *by* being born of the Virgin Mary. He "made himself of no reputation, and took upon him the form of a servant, and was made in the likeness of men" (Philippians 2:7). Mary cannot be ignored; we need to think about this: no Eve no fall of man; no Mary, no salvation of man. We see clearly that Mary is integral to our salvation, while *not* being at all the one who saves us. She is greatly important, and she should be held in the highest esteem, understood rightly as our Church Fathers understood her. She is the New Eve.

Mary as the New Ark

Below are some wonderful quotes from the earliest Church Fathers, who made the glorious observation that Mary is not only the New Eve but also the New Ark.

"To whom among all creatures shall I compare you, O Virgin? You are greater than them all O [Ark of the] Covenant, clothed with purity instead of gold! You are the ark in which is found the golden vessel containing the true manna, that is, the flesh in which divinity resides." (St. Athanasius of Alexandria, *Homily of the Papyrus of Turin*)

"Let us chant the melody that has been taught us by the inspired harp of David, and say, 'Arise, O Lord, into thy rest; thou, and the ark of thy sanctuary.' For the Holy Virgin is in truth an ark, wrought with gold both within and without, that has received the whole treasury of the sanctuary." (St. Gregory the Wonderworker, *Homily on the Annunciation to the Holy Virgin Mary*)

The situation here is much like the situation with the New Adam (explicitly conveyed in the text of the Bible) and the New Eve (not explicitly stated or even derived necessarily from the Bible, but reasonably concluded by the great theologians of old). In the Gospels, Jesus made a connection between the physical Temple in Jerusalem, made with stones and human hands on the one hand, and His body, made of flesh, on the other. "Jesus answered and said unto them, Destroy this temple, and in three days I will raise it up. Then said the Jews, Forty and six years was this temple in building, and wilt thou rear it up in three days? But spake of the temple of his body" (John 2:19-21). And so, although the Bible does not explicitly call Jesus the "New Temple," He is in fact the New Temple, just as He is the New Adam.

This conclusion is proven nowhere else better than in the book of Hebrews, which was written for a Jewish audience, one that best would have understood the significance of the teaching of the physical temple being replaced by the New Temple, which is Christ:

> 11. But Christ being come an high priest of good things to come, by a greater and more perfect tabernacle, not made with hands, that is to say, not of this building;
> 12. Neither by the blood of goats and calves, but by his own blood he entered in once into the holy place, having obtained eternal redemption for us.
> 13. For if the blood of bulls and of goats, and the ashes of an heifer sprinkling the

unclean, sanctifieth to the purifying of the flesh:

14. How much more shall the blood of Christ, who through the eternal Spirit offered himself without spot to God, purge your conscience from dead works to serve the living God?

15. And for this cause he is the mediator of the new testament, that by means of death, for the redemption of the transgressions that were under the first testament, they which are called might receive the promise of eternal inheritance.

23. It was therefore necessary that the patterns of things in the heavens should be purified with these; but the heavenly things themselves with better sacrifices than these...

24. For Christ is not entered into the holy places made with hands, which are the figures of the true; but into heaven itself, now to appear in the presence of God for us:

25. For yet that he should offer himself often, as the high priest entereth into the holy place every year with blood of others;

26. For then must he often have suffered since the foundation of the world: but now once in the end of the world hath he

appeared to put away sin by the sacrifice of himself.

Hebrews 9:11-15, 23-26

Likewise, seeing that the New Covenant brought with it a new understanding of heavenly things, raising the carnal, physical, visible world into the realm of the invisible, spiritual, Godly world, it stands to reason that even the Ark itself, made with human hands, nested inside of the old Temple like Adam's rib, should have a spiritual corollary in the salvation story. That corollary is Mary.

The Ark contained the tablets of the Law, written by the finger of God, Who is the Word ("and the Word was with God, and the Word was God"—John 1:1). And so the Ark could be likened to Mary's womb, pregnant with the Word ("and the Word was made flesh, and dwelt among us"—John 1:14). The Ark was so holy that if anyone dared to touch it, they would immediately perish, as we read:

> 4. And they brought it out of the house of Abinadab which *was* at Gibeah, accompanying the ark of God: and Ahio went before the ark.

5. And David and all the house of Israel played before the LORD on all manner of *instruments made of* fir wood, even on harps, and on psalteries, and on timbrels, and on cornets, and on cymbals.
6. And when they came to Nachon's threshingfloor, Uzzah put forth *his hand* to the ark of God, and took hold of it; for the oxen shook *it.*
7. And the anger of the LORD was kindled against Uzzah; and God smote him there for *his* error; and there he died by the ark of God
8. And David was displeased, because the LORD had made a breach upon Uzzah: and he called the name of the place Perezuzzah to this day
9. And David was afraid of the LORD that day, and said, **How shall the ark of the LORD come to me**?

2 Samuel. 6:4-9

Not only does this establish the holiness of the Ark, but it also gives us a very important clue in the last verse as to the connection between the Ark and Mary. The same sort of phrasing that David used in reference to the Ark is used by Elisabeth when Mary came to visit her, but with one essential difference. St. Elisabeth asked, "And whence *is* this to me, that the mother of my Lord should come to me? For, lo, as soon as the voice of thy salutation sounded in mine ears, the babe leaped in my womb for joy" (Luke 1:43-44). Once again, we see a happy inversion: whereas the Law and the Ark brought forth for David and his company both death and fear, the New Ark, who is Mary, brings forth life and joy. Thus it takes no stretch of the imagination to conceive of Mary as the New Ark, even *holier* than the former likeness, which was just a shadow, but bringing with her the joyous gift of Salvation instead of the letter of the Law which brings only death.

> 5. For when we were in the flesh, the motions of sins, which were by the law, did work in our members to bring forth fruit unto death.
> 6. But now we are delivered from the law, that being dead wherein we were held; that we should serve in newness of spirit, and not in the oldness of the letter.
>
> *Romans 7:6-7*

Having been brought up in the Lutheran Church in my early years, and having had many, many conversations with my Lutheran mother in my adulthood about various biblical subjects, I look at what I have set forth in these pages thus far and am immediately reminded of Luther's famous saying: "Scripture interprets Scripture." Surprisingly to some, all we need to know about Mary comes straight from Sacred Scripture, either directly and plainly, or by inference, or by parallel or analogy. Where sincere Christians have gone off the rails with respect to Mary is not so much their understanding of her as it is how they *apply* that understanding in practice, as we shall investigate later.

Mary as the Queen Mother

A lot of people probably wonder why Roman Catholics believe in "to Jesus, through Mary," if they want their prayers to be heard.[2] They do this for many reasons.

---

[2] The "to Jesus, through Mary" concept is much older than *True Devotion to the Blessed Virgin* by Saint Louis-Marie Grignion de Montefort (b. 1673-1716), who is often considered to have been the father of this Marian devotion. In fact, it can be traced back to

One is because of a devotional practice that gained favor—and fervor—during the Middle Ages, a time when there was a very heavy emphasis on the Christ of the Last Judgment. Mary was appealed to for intercessory prayers because Jesus was viewed as more of an angry judge than as a friend or brother.[3] One of the underpinnings of the idea that Mary could gain favor with Christ the King on our behalf derives from relatively obscure biblical texts, but ones that Catholics *can* legitimately point to as the basis of their belief and practice.

Catholics see Mary as the Queen Mother over the house of David. The idea that one of Mary's titles or functions is that of "Queen Mother" is probably entirely foreign to any Christian outside of the Roman Catholic church, but it is not only a biblical idea but also a historical one. It has to do with the important and powerful role that the mother of the king played in the court of

---

the writings of Catholic theologians going all the way back to at least the seventh century.

[3] Even though Roman Catholics today of the Novus Ordo persuasion have gone much too far in the other direction, choosing "accompaniment" and shying away from any talk of judgment, the practice of reciting Rosaries has never ceased with them.

the kings of Israel and Judah. Anyone who is familiar with Christian art over the centuries has likely seen paintings depicting the Coronation of Mary. The Coronation of Mary also happens to be one of the various contemplations involving the Rosary. Learning more about Mary as Queen Mother should at least lend a greater understanding of what the coronation image means.

The word for Queen Mother in Hebrew is *Gebirah*, which means Great Lady. According to the rubrics of the king's court in the time of Israel and Judah, the *Gebirah* held great sway over the kings in the Davidic line, as exemplified in the following passage:

> 13. Now Adonijah, the son of Haggith, went to Bathsheba, Solomon's mother. Bathsheba asked him, "Do you come peacefully?" He answered, "Yes, peacefully."
> 14. Then he added, "I have something to say to you." "You may say it," she replied.
> 15. As you know," he said, "the kingdom was mine. All Israel looked to me as their king. But things changed, and the kingdom has gone to my brother; for it has come to him from the LORD.

16. Now I have one request to make of you. Do not refuse me." "You may make it," she said.

17. So he continued, "Please ask King Solomon—he will not refuse you—to give me Abishag the Shunammite as my wife."

18. "Very well," Bathsheba replied, "I will speak to the king for you."

19. When Bathsheba went to King Solomon to speak to him for Adonijah, the king stood up to meet her, bowed down to her and sat down on his throne. He had a throne brought for the king's mother, and she sat down at his right hand.

20. I have one small request to make of you," she said. "Do not refuse me." The king replied, "Make it, my mother; I will not refuse you."

1 Kings 2:13-20

There are a few interesting things to take note of in this passage concerning the Queen Mother, Bathsheba, in relation to King Solomon. First, Adonijah does not go directly to the king, so as to avoid the king's wrath. Instead he appeals to Bathsheba, who acts as intercessor between Adonijah and King Solomon. Second, although Solomon ultimately *does* refuse Bathsheba's request, as was his right to do so as king, his default response was "I will not refuse you." It should be noted that a throne was brought for Queen Bathsheba, that she sat down at King Solomon's right hand, and that the king "stood up to meet her" and "bowed down to her." Clearly the Queen Mother had tremendous power and authority in the king's household, and she had a direct line to the king's ear. It is in this capacity as intercessor that Mary began to be seen more and more as an intercessor (i.e., Mediatrix) between us and God, second only to Christ as Mediator.

Many Christians are appalled by the idea of Mary being considered Mediatrix, using the tenet of *Sola Scriptura* to point to the verse that states clearly, "For there is one God, and one mediator between God and men, the man Christ Jesus; Who gave himself a ransom for all, to be testified in due time" (1 Timothy 2:5-6). But the Church Fathers dating all the way back to at least the 4th century began to discern that Mary, while not being "*The* Mediator" did play a mediating role in salvation, thus giving her the title of Mediatrix. For example, a prayer attributed to St. Ephrem the Syrian (4th century) includes the declaration: "after the mediator [Christ], you [Mary] are the mediatrix of the whole world."

But "Mediatrix" can mean different things. In one respect it can be said that Mary truly was a unique mediator between God and man in that by her faith and obedience, the Incarnation was able to take place, and hence the Crucifixion, the Resurrection, and our Redemption from the bondage of sin and death. And so in this sense, she *did* play a part in our salvation. In another respect we can think of her as a mediator in that she is the Queen Mother, being that Christ Jesus is from the line of David, and she has her Son's ear in all things. This doesn't mean that He *must* obey every one of her requests, as we saw in the above passage from 1 Kings, but it does mean that He will pay close attention to them. A good example of this can be found in the description of the first miracle recorded in the Gospels.

> 3. And when they wanted wine, the mother of Jesus saith unto him, They have no wine.

4. Jesus saith unto her, Woman, what have I to do with thee? mine hour is not yet come.
5. His mother saith unto the servants, Whatsoever he saith unto you, do it.
6. And there were set there six waterpots of stone, after the manner of the purifying of the Jews, containing two or three firkins apiece.
7. Jesus saith unto them, Fill the waterpots with water. And they filled them up to the brim.
8. And he saith unto them, Draw out now, and bear unto the governor of the feast. And they bare it.

John 2:3-8

In this story, Mary intercedes for the wedding party and the host, seeing to it that they are not ashamed or their party ruined. She appeals to her Son to discretely perform a miracle that day, knowing already not only that He could do this miracle but that He *would* do it, even though she also knew that His time had not yet come—that He was not prepared yet to start making His identity known among the people. Yet, she knew her Son so well that despite His verbal resistance, she turned to the servants anyway, and she confidently instructed them to do whatever Jesus told them to do. Here Mary is playing a very active role working alongside Jesus to help her fellow man in a concrete way, and yet in a way that glorifies God at the same time.

So it should seem clear that the case against giving Mary the due reverence that she deserves is not as solid as some may think. In other words, who else in the Bible had this type of influence over Jesus? I don't think we can find anyone else. We could look at it another way. Imagine a young woman was interested in a young man, and the two began to date and soon fell in love. Now imagine the young man wanted to marry this young woman, so he decided to bring her home to his mother, whom he adored. His father had passed away, and his siblings had already gone off in different directions. He lived just with his mother, who in turn adored her son. Now imagine the son brings his soon-to-be fiancée to his home, and she walks in and ignores the young man's mother. She talks over her and looks through her. She wants only to be with and talk to the young man, as though his mother weren't even there. Imagine how insulted both the mother and the young man would be if this young woman behaved in such a disgraceful manner! This is what people are doing when all they want to do is make a beeline for Christ while ignoring or discrediting the Blessed Mother—similar to those who insult the Church in favor of a "personal relationship with Christ." We need to think about it. We *say* that we believe in every word of the Bible, but when we learn that St. Elisabeth, who spoke by the power of the Holy Spirit, was in awe that the mother of her Lord should come to *her*, and when we learn that Mary prophesied that all generations would henceforth call her blessed—and yet we don't *do* so—one wonders whether our anti-Catholic biases have put us on dangerous ground. Have we gone too far?

There is a reason why Protestants have put up a barrier against Mary, and that reason is perfectly understandable. Many Roman Catholics have ruined what could otherwise have been perfectly good and sound Marian teaching by taking those ideas to dangerous extremes. Is there a *via media* for Traditional Anglicans?

First we should consider where the line might be drawn between reasonable contemplation of truths about Mary and unreasonable extremes concerning Mary. In the preceding pages of this article, I have outlined reasons why certain beliefs about Mary have formed over the first several centuries of the Church. All of these beliefs are rooted in Scripture, whether directly or indirectly, and all of them are truly Catholic because up until shortly after the first millennium they were believed "everywhere, always, by all"—a mark, or test, of catholicity as expressed by St. Vincent of Lérins in his *Commonitorium*.

It wasn't until the second millennium that concepts such as "Mediatrix" began to morph into new terms for Mary that really began to push the envelope. One such term is "Co-Redemptrix," which surfaced in the late Middle Ages and gained popularity among the Franciscans, though contested by the Dominicans. It wasn't a big leap from that to Mary being conceived as the "Immaculate Conception" in that she was thought to be conceived without the "stain" of original sin—another idea made popular among the Franciscans and opposed by the Dominicans, also in the late Middle Ages. Great medieval theologians such as St. Thomas Aquinas and St. Bernard of

Clairvaux did not support (or at least not fully) the idea of the Immaculate Conception as it was being developed, although Catholic apologists today have been busy trying to explain away the cognitive dissonance that comes with the fact that not every Catholic saint believed what later became dogma.

Thus, later developments that moved the needle far from center on Mary did not pass the test of catholicity: these new beliefs were *not* believed "everywhere, always, by all." A new cult of Mary began to emerge, complete with visions, apparitions, and new prayers and sacramental observations to be followed (the Rosary, the scapular, the Miraculous Medal, etc.). Marianism began to overtake religious practice to such an extent that the Immaculate Conception was made into Roman Catholic dogma in 1854:

> We declare, pronounce, and define that the doctrine which holds that the most Blessed Virgin Mary, in the first instance of her conception, by a singular grace and privilege granted by Almighty God, in view of the merits of Jesus Christ, the Saviour of the human race, was preserved free from all stain of original sin, is a doctrine revealed by God and therefore to

be believed firmly and constantly by all the faithful.

Pope Pius IX, Ineffabilis Deus, 1854

To stay a Roman Catholic, one was now compelled by this papal bull to believe that Mary was conceived without original sin—in short, that she was sinless—with the veiled implication that not to believe as such would mean excommunication. There is something in Roman Catholicism called *latae sententiae* excommunication, which means automatic excommunication without the need for a sentence to be handed down by an ecclesiastical court. Grounds for a *latae sententiae* excommunication could be being an apostate from the faith, a heretic, or a schismatic. The effect of making the Immaculate Conception dogma is to put all Roman Catholics in a state of excommunication if they do not believe it.

Now why would a concept like the Immaculate Conception need to be made into dogma in the first place if it were believed, "everywhere, always, by all"? This shows that this teaching does not arc back the beginning of the Church, nor does it find any justification in the Bible. In short, it is a relatively modern teaching that did not begin to gain traction until the later Middle Ages, along with the Rosary as we know it today. If you take a broad view, these practices and beliefs are innovations: they cannot hold sway over the minds of any Christian.

How the Immaculate Conception became a teaching in the first place has much more to do with misunderstandings about Original Sin than it does about Mary. All the mental gyrations that led up to the adoption of the Immaculate Conception dogma stemmed from the idea that Christ could not be sinless if His mother was conceived in sin. Therefore Mary must *not* have been conceived in sin, but instead her conception had to have been "immaculate," as it says in this famous Miraculous Medal prayer, "O Mary, conceived without sin, pray for us who have recourse to thee"—the words of the prayer allegedly given to Saint Catherine Labouré in a vision.

It would take a great deal of time to unpack how the Roman Catholic Church went off course in the area of the Immaculate Conception, or to fully explain how wrongful it is to believe that any person other than Christ was *conceived sinless*, or how easy it is to fall into a kind of "worshipfulness," if not actual worship, of such a person while convincing oneself that one isn't actually doing that.

Roman Catholics aver that they are not giving *latria* to Mary but only *hyperdulia*, with *latria* being worship, reserved for God alone, and *hyperdulia* being the highest degree of veneration, reserved for the Blessed Mother alone, above all other saints. However, the line between *hyperdulia* and *latria* becomes merely academic the moment one believes that Mary was conceived without sin. Why? Because it veers into direct contradiction with Sacred Scripture, and that is where no Christian wants to go. It also elevates Mary beyond what is lawful. As Traditional Anglicans, we must also steer completely clear of such teaching, as it violates Article XV of the Thirty-Nine Articles, which declares that Christ alone is without sin, as well as the Bible itself.

Jesus "committed no sin" (1 Peter 2:22), "knew no sin" (2 Corinthians 5:21), and was "without sin" (Hebrews 4:15). Nobody else in the Bible is referred to in this way. In fact, we only know the *opposite* to be true: "For all have sinned, and come short of the glory of God; Being justified freely by his grace through the redemption that is in Christ Jesus" (Romans 3:23-24). Mary herself confesses, "my spirit hath rejoiced in God my **Saviour**" (Luke 1:16). In fact, if Mary was conceived without the stain of any original sin, however that may be defined (e.g., inherited stain of sin, imputed guilt of Adam), then that would mean that her parents and their parents up to X number of generations going back to Adam also would have had the same quality, but of course that idea is ridiculous. Instead, what does make sense is yet another "middle way" in our understanding of how it can be that Mary was both born in the same way as you and me *and* a spotless vessel for the Holy Spirit to descend upon her and cause her to conceive God Himself. How can both things be true at the same time?

It would take too many pages to sum up all that has been written on this topic, or how and why the doctrine of the Immaculate Conception came to be. Put succinctly, the most reasonable way to reconcile this dilemma is to simply look at Luke 1:35:

And the angel answered and said unto her, The Holy Ghost shall come upon thee, and the **power of the Highest shall overshadow thee: therefore** also that **holy thing** which shall be born of thee shall be called the Son of God.

It can thus most reasonably be concluded that the Blessed Mother was *made* entirely immaculate in body and soul by the power of the Holy Spirit having overshadowed her, after she willingly consented to become the Mother of God, and that "therefore" she was able to bear the "holy thing" in her womb, being a fitting vessel for the Word to be made flesh.

If Mary was made immaculate by the Holy Spirit, then how can we explain the observance of the Purification of Mary, which we commemorate every Candlemas along with the Presentation of Our Lord? Doesn't this event prove that Mary was just an ordinary sinner like you and me? No, it does not.

As we can know that Mary is the New Eve by inference from the direct biblical teaching that Jesus is the New Adam, we can know the answer to this puzzle by analogy, noting Jesus's response to John the Baptist when He came to him to be baptized:

14. But John forbad him, saying, I have need to be baptized of thee, and comest thou to me?

15. And Jesus answering said unto him, Suffer it to be so now: for **thus it becometh us to fulfil all righteousness**. Then he suffered him.

Matthew 3:14-15

Another argument that could be made in an attempt to disprove the idea that Mary was made immaculate by the Holy Spirit might go like this: If Mary was made immaculate, then why didn't God simply make *all* of us immaculate, thus bypassing the need for Christ to suffer death on the cross? Wouldn't that have been easier and less painful for all? The reasons why this could never have happened are clear: (1) only *one* human being, a virgin, could have been chosen to be the *Theotokos*, since one can only be physically born of one mother, and thus only one human being could have been made immaculate for that purpose; (2) our redemption and salvation *required* the Incarnation of the Word through Mary, because (3) it is only by the shedding of *blood* that we can be saved—not by the blood of "calves and of goats," but only through the most precious blood of Christ, as we read:

22. And almost all things are by the law purged with blood; and **without shedding of blood is no remission**.
23. It was therefore **necessary** that the patterns of things in the heavens should be purified with these; but the heavenly things themselves with better sacrifices than these.

Hebrews 9:22-23

Therefore, Mary couldn't have been "conceived without sin" because that would have changed her ontology, putting her on equal footing with the Lord Jesus Christ. If anyone can be said to be the Immaculate Conception at all, it is Christ, not Mary. It is also not necessary for one to believe that Mary never committed a sin a single day in her life, whether before her *fiat* or after Christ was born. This question is irrelevant. The only questions relevant for orthodoxy with respect to Mary and Christ are these:

- Was Christ the only-begotten Son of God, conceived by the Holy Ghost of the Virgin Mary and become man? (Yes; see First Ecumenical Council; Apostle's Creed; Article II of the Thirty-Nine Articles of Religion.)

75

- Is Mary the Mother of God, or *Theotokos*? (Yes; see the conclusions of the Third Ecumenical Council.)

- Is Christ fully God and fully man? (Yes; see the conclusions of the Fourth Ecumenical Council.)

- May we venerate icons of the Virgin Mary and Christ? (Yes; see the conclusion of the Seventh Ecumenical Council.)

- Do we believe in the Communion of Saints? (Yes; see the Apostle's Creed.)

- Does the Communion of Saints entail that intercessory prayer is permitted? (No; see Article XXII on the Invocation of Saints, Thirty-Nine Articles.)

If we desire to have a closer relationship with the holy saints, and especially Mary[4], a middle-way option for Anglicans is to ask God to ask the saints to pray for us. In this way, we avoid engaging in intercessory prayer, which is proscribed in the Thirty-Nine Articles of Religion. Instead, we could

---

[4] Note: This may be desired not only by Anglicans, but also particularly by Christians moving out of Catholicism and Orthodoxy and into the Anglican Church, a need of which we should first be aware, and then be attentive to pastorally.

ask God to activate the Communion of Saints in heaven to pray on our behalf.

The questions in the above bullet points have been settled long ago. For instance, with regard to the veneration of icons, at the Seventh Ecumenical Council, the ruling came down in favor of it as follows (and Protestants are supposed to accept *all seven* of the first Seven Ecumenical Councils):

> As the sacred and life-giving cross is everywhere set up as a symbol, so also should the images of Jesus Christ, the Virgin Mary, the holy angels, as well as those of the saints and other pious and holy men be embodied in the manufacture of sacred vessels, tapestries, vestments, etc., and exhibited on the walls of churches, in the homes, and in all conspicuous places, by the roadside and everywhere, to be revered by all who might see them. For the more they are contemplated, the more they move to fervent memory of their prototypes. Therefore, it is proper to accord to them a fervent and reverent veneration, not, however, the veritable adoration which, according to our faith, belongs to the Divine Being alone—for the honor

accorded to the image passes over to its prototype, and whoever venerate the image venerate in it the reality of what is there represented.

Second Council of Nicaea, Seventh Session, October 13, 787)

Conclusion

I have spent a great deal of time thinking about Mary and contemplating who she is, and what she represents, to the Church. I took my time in the Roman Catholic Church extremely seriously, and I learned a great deal from her and benefitted from her, even though in the end I had to say goodbye to her. But as I mentioned before, we are all like dogs on God's leash, and we pick up things along the way that stick, good and beautiful things that God allows us to keep close to our hearts, even as He pulls us back again, and He and we continue on our journey together.

One of those beautiful things that I learned as a Roman Catholic was a deep love for Mary and an appreciation of what she did for us—the critical part she played in the salvation story. Time does not allow for me to get into various Roman Catholic contemplations and devotions centering around her, but one that I happen to love deeply is the depiction of Mary with seven swords piercing her heart. That image is called Our Lady of Sorrows. Perhaps some may view the devotion to the image as excessive, but the inspiration for it is not. It comes from Luke yet again, the most Marian of all the Gospels:

> 34. And Simeon blessed them and said unto Mary His mother, "Behold, this Child is set for the fall and rising again of many in Israel, and for a sign which shall be spoken against
> 35. (yea, **a sword shall pierce through thy own soul** also), that the thoughts of many hearts may be revealed.

> *Luke 2:34-35*

I'm a mother. I can't imagine being pregnant with the only child I will ever have, a baby boy, knowing that by the time that precious baby being carried in my own womb becomes 33 years old, he will be rejected by everyone, spat upon, whipped, tortured, and crucified, dying an agonizing and lonely death—what's more, knowing that I'd witness it all as it was happening, suffering incalculable emotional pain, knowing that I could not help him or take the cruelty away, not even for one second. Mary experienced the kind of pain and isolation that would be intolerable for any woman, but she did it "full of grace," always staying the humble handmaiden of the Lord.

Now then, is it right to ask in the song, "Mary, did you know...."? No, it's wrong. Mary knew all that would befall her and her Son, for as Elisabeth prophesied, "And blessed is she that believed: for there shall be a performance of those things **which were told her from the Lord**" (Luke 1:45). Mary literally united with God the Holy Spirit, becoming His bride. The Holy Spirit, in turn, made her completely pure, rendering her a most pure vessel to allow Christ to be conceived in her immaculate womb. The Holy Spirit told Mary all that was to come. Her special union with God can never be matched.

What is the right attitude toward Mary? We cannot—*we must not*—ignore her, let alone slight her, as some do, while on the other hand we cannot make her so important that we overshadow Christ Himself—in essence worshiping her while claiming not to be.

Can there be a balance between those two extremes in the life of a Traditional Anglican? Anglicans are well aware of the tipping point beyond which the Roman Catholic church went off the rails on the subject of Mary, but let's not throw the baby out with the bathwater! The Catholics are more right about Mary than they are wrong about her in theory, but in practice their heavy emphasis on Marian visions, private revelations, apparitions, and prayers to Mary eclipse our relationship with Christ and artificially make the focus of our faith almost entirely on Mary—particularly in private life. I have seen it, and I have lived it. I know whereof I speak.

Having walked in Orthodox circles for several years before entering the Anglican Church first as a parishioner and then as a Deaconess, I can say that the Orthodox church seems to strike a better balance with regard to Mary—though certainly some have veered off into a dependency on "streaming icons" and the like. No Orthodox Christian should need a streaming icon to support their faith (much like no Roman Catholic should need signs, visions, apparitions, bleeding Hosts, and the like to remain faithful and obedient to Christ—Who, it should be said plainly right now, is "**the** head of the body, the church" [Colossians 1:18], not the Pope of Rome).

One should consider such things to be *adiaphora*, or a matter of indifference. Such beliefs and practices aren't enough to make one a heretic, and conversely *not* believing them or doing them doesn't make one a heretic either—irrespective of certain puffed up claims on both sides. There is common ground to be shared among all Catholic Christians who share the same beliefs in common as expressed minimally and conservatively by, for example, the Apostle's Creed. Maybe some of the aforementioned things are real, or maybe none of them are; everyone should be aware, however, that some of them are fake, since opportunists and charlatans have abounded since the first days of the Church, as the Apostle John informed us: the spirit of antichrist "even now already is it in the world" (1 John 4:3).

But I will say this: there are icons everywhere in the Orthodox churches of Jesus, Mary, the Holy Angels, and the saints, and those icons *are* part of our rich Catholic Christian tradition, whose use is fully supported by the Seventh Ecumenical Council, which all Christians are bound to accept as valid for understanding the Christian faith.

As to whether we should actually *pray to* Mary, in the sense of asking her to intercede on our behalf (e.g., "pray for us sinners, now, and at the hour of our death" in the Rosary), the Thirty-Nine Articles of Religion teach that we should not be communicating with the saints at all: we are only to *pray for* the dead.

There is no evidence either way that the saints can or cannot hear us, or that they can or cannot pray for a person if that person were to turn to them. There are arguments that can be made for and against whether saints have any awareness at all of what is going on here on earth: some say that because of their *theosis* with God, becoming like God, they share God's awareness of all things. Others say that isn't likely to be possible, as there must be a great gulf between heaven and earth, and the saints have no awareness or remembrance anymore of what is going on down here, as they are living in paradise.

As for me, I believe the Communion of Saints that we confess in our Creed is a communion of the saints on earth with each other on earth, as well as a continual communion of saints on earth with the saints in heaven, and that this is happening at all times and always, whether we are aware of it or not. I believe that saints exist in both realms, rejecting entirely the process of canonization of saints, as performed by the Roman Catholic Church. There are saints among us today and everywhere, and they are the whole body of believers on earth, as every epistle makes clear—all of them written for and addressed to none other than the saints. All it means to be a saint is to be holy, set apart, chosen by God for a special purpose. Together with the saints in heaven, we are united in praise and thanksgiving to God, mutually praying for one another, as we do for the "faithful departed."

Because I also believe in *theosis,* I believe that Mary and all the saints *do* have an awareness of what is going on here on earth, that they care for us, and that they are praying for us, whether we ask for their prayers or not, or whether we see evidence of such prayers or not. We cannot see God "as he is" but they *already* see Him now. "Beloved, now are we the sons of God, and it doth not yet appear what we shall be: but we know that, when He shall appear, **we shall be like him**; for we shall **see him as He is**" (1 John 3:2).

A right understanding of Mary is not merely a matter of *adiaphora*—more a matter of indifference, as already defined— but rather *theologoumenon*: a theological opinion that, when properly and legitimately offered, can be strongly backed by biblical evidence while at the same time not being strictly binding for the faithful.

Therefore, brethren, I see that it is no robbery against God to have a close Communion-of-Saints relationship with the Mother of God, the Blessed Mother, that Great Lady, Mary. I believe that since Mary is Jesus's mother, this makes her the highest of all of the saints, for through her alone among women were we redeemed by the mystery of the Incarnation. Since she is the mother of my Savior, she is my mother too, through the adoption of sonship by the Father through Christ Jesus. And if she is my mother, I should give her all the love and honor due to her. I exhort my fellow Anglicans to be reminded of Jesus's teaching that the spiritual and invisible are more perfect than the physical and visible. And so "Honour thy father and thy mother: that thy days may be long upon the land which the LORD thy God giveth thee" (Exodus 20:12).

www.ingramcontent.com/pod-product-compliance
Lightning Source LLC
Chambersburg PA
CBHW060346130626
46553CB00003B/1111